A Poet's Journey
By
Justin Young

Dedicated to my late grandfather James Andrew Young, II

Justin Young
Copyright 2012
All Rights Reserved
Printed in the United States of America
Heart2Heart Publishing
P.O. Box 3573
Oak Brook, IL 60523
708-254-5232

ISBN 0-9710558-7-4

Thank You

First and foremost I have to give the majority of my thanks to my mother. She has been by my side through each and everything that has gone on in my life. She is my heart and I love her to death. Second, I want to thank my father too for always supporting me with whatever I wanted to do. I can always go to my dad whenever I just need to get my mind off of things. I love being able to just sit and listen to him give me all types of advice, he is the greatest father on the planet in my eyes and I want him to know that. I want to thank all of my brothers and sisters for being by my side. I know I can always depend on my siblings to help me out with anything I need them to.

I give thanks to my Auntie Raisha for always being there for me too. And last but not least I have to give thanks to my grandparents. My grandparents are my escape from everything. I've spent countless nights at their house because it is so relaxing and peaceful. Everything is so calm. My Grandpa Herman would always talk to me about a variety of things over a cup of coffee while out for breakfast, or just at home relaxing. He has always inspired me to want to do better and I want him to realize the impact that he has had on my life. He would always tell me I could be running my own business and making all of the money I could ever dream of.

Overall I just want to thank everyone who was there for me through my struggle, and who is still with me now. You all are appreciated, thank you so much!

It takes a village to raise a child
- African proverb

Through a Mother's Eyes

Have you ever been in a position where you felt helpless or had that uneasy feeling in the pit of your stomach that you would rather die? I have! It was the moment I came home to find out my son had taken a mixture of pills in an attempt to end his own life. There were so many emotions raging within me; ANGER, FEAR, SORROW, and the most intense FAILURE. Angry that he would be so selfish, fearful that his attempt would be successful not knowing what he had taken, sorrow because I could not stop the pain he was experiencing, and failure because there had to be something wrong with me if my child thought life was so bad that it wasn't worth living anymore.

I took all of those emotions and forged a bond with my son and war on anything and anyone who would dare to stand in the way of his journey to recovery. I promised him that "NO MATTER WHAT," we were going to make it through this. And boy did he test that promise. Anxiety ridden every time he would leave the house, sleepless nights because I would check, and double-check, and triple-check that I had not forgotten any medicine or aspirin bottles laying around the house, countless trips to therapy, and many fights because of the varying mood swings and episodes of the major depression he was experiencing. It all then began to take its toll, the guilt that I should have parented differently, the self-pity because I didn't act on the changes I saw him in earlier, and the exhaustion to keep smiling so that he would never know the weight of the pain I was carrying for the both of us.

While physically to the outsider's eye it appeared he wasn't going to make it, through my eyes I knew there was no other option! I was willing to stay on that journey with him until he was able to see his way out. Thank you to my amazing husband James and my children Jacquelynne and Jaymes who loved both of us enough to hold us up in prayer, pickup chores around the house, and lend a listening ear through it all.

Justin, I love you, you are my heart and I always knew that your journey would lead you to greatness.

~ Your Ma

The Journey Begins

First Signs

My mind is going crazy and I swear I need to vent
And so I take this pen and these poems I invent
My feelings being masked
And my life is rearranged
A thousand questions asked
Not a single answer gained
So these questions still remain
And my mind just goes insane
While these questions keep on floating in and all around my brain
And as I slowly lose sanity
And try to stay sane
I become a victim of vanity
I'm amazed
As my world begins to turn
Some sanity is what I yearn
And I slowly start to fade
As my life begins to burn

Flowing Thoughts

Running out of rhymes
Slowly running out of my mind
These poems aren't a pastime
It's what's helping me survive
It's what's keeping me alive
Even when I'm losing faith
Feel like I'm getting left behind
In a slow but steady race
I need to speed up the pace
Before I'm gone without a trace
Before I become all forgotten
Like a loner out in space
So I decided I'm going to zone
A thousand poems on my phone
Thinking, will my wordplay leave some thoughts inside their dome?
So much stuff I've done wrong
But then again I've done stuff right
All the fights, arguments, and going sleepless through the night
Will they miss me when I'm gone?
Probably not but it's alright.

The Renewal

The clock is winding down
His body is in the suit that's in the casket in the ground
I see the young boy as he calmly faces death
Rapid heart beats
His heart is thumping out his chest
So I turn my music low
Grab my phone and start to flow
And I wait for him to die
Like a bomb waits to blow
And I know that once he goes it won't completely end the show
He told me that he's got a very long journey he must go
And as I stand upon the face of the boy in preparation
I become truly astounded by the problems that he's facing
As I stared upon the mirror and I looked me in the eye
I told him there's a new you
The old one had to die
If you read this poem carefully you'll slowly start to see
That the boy I'm talking about was the old version of me.

Regret and Sorrow

We all speak words out of anger
But the wrong words can leave relationships in danger
And you become embarrassed when you get to thinking about
All the people you had snapped on that you couldn't live without
And you start to feel the sorrow
All the love they let you borrow
And you fuss and break their heart
Then you take it back tomorrow
When you know right off the bat
That you really do not hate them
But you screamed and told them that
And then they began to believe
Because the message they received was that you wanted them to leave
And then they leave and you beg for one more try
And this process never stops until you grow old and die
And your spirits in the sky
But your body is down below
And once again you're asking why
But this time you will never know.

I Should've

I should've let you go
I should've told you no
I should've let you know.
I should've let my heart hide
Because love can't be revived
But love is still alive
So when will it arrive?
I should've gave a scream
I should've came between
I should've let you cry
But this love just wouldn't die

I looked you in the eye
And slowly wiped the tear away
I gave a soft kiss

Welcome to a new day
I should've left you alone
Instead I brought you to my home
I should've done it right
But everything is wrong
I should've turned to leave
I should've let me breath
I should've set me free
I should've been me.
I should've followed my heart
I should've right from the start
I should've lived with it.

I should've but I didn't.

Life's Fight

My brain is filled with thoughts
From all the battles that I've fought
All the lessons got taught
And all the knowledge it brought
Along from past years
So many hidden secrets
And even more hidden tears
Went from falling in love
To getting drunk off beers
To getting higher than doves
And beating up all my peers
To slowly thinking things through
And started to change my crew
To staying out in the streets
Ready to be deceased
And all those nights I would cry
Feeling like I would die
But never letting them people see the pain in my eyes
I'm a star in the sky
I just need help shining bright
So I can make it through the night
And survive Life's Fight.

Life at Stake

I feel the blood as it's flowing through my veins
A bunch of heavy thoughts are being carried through my brain
And lately all I'm thinking about is not going insane
But I'm insane in the brain that's been trying to keep me sane
And it will never be the same because my mind just can't be tamed
And I'm thinking of the days when my sun shined bright
And at all the pretty stars that used to shine bright in the night
But now my nights turn into fights
And now the stars are no longer in sight
And now I think of recent plights
Exhausted in a restless fright
And all I want to do is get away and take a flight
I swear I'll make it through
But if I don't just know I tried with all my might
I don't know how much more my soul can take
Because I'm gambling my mental health
My life is now at stake

Summer Sadness

Spend my days in mourning
Wake up sadly in the morning
Wish the sun would go away
And give me back the moon
Take away all of the stars
And just replace it with my doom
Let the darkness shadow over me
Connect it with my gloom
Trying to sweep away these feelings
But can't seem to find the broom
So my spirit stays shaken
Sometimes I just can't seem to take it
Who creates these pitch black feelings?
Can they tell me if I'll make it?
Nothing I can do but wait
All the sins I shall forsake
Because in the midst of all the waiting
I hope its peace I come across
I truly need the relaxation
And the pain to be at ease
So I can just relax and enjoy the summer breeze

Random Thought

Reminiscing on the past
It seems to be a war
A moment that will forever last
More rain will start to pour
It pours on the poor who can't find an open door
Because no one will accept them
They live life like it's a chore
I hope that we all come together
In reality, we'll never
But I won't let facts kill my dream
No more letting little things come between

Zone

Tears filling up like water in a cup
His past came so fast, so hard, so abrupt
I wish that I could intervene
I wish to interrupt
I wish something would come between
And make life less rough
But if it gets less rough then I get less tough
And I want to stay tough
Even though I know that being tough just ain't enough
Most people lust for love
But it's me that loves the lust
So I put the love beneath and I keep the lust above
Never let them get to me
Keep your mind strong
Because they believing that you are going to break
But their beliefs are all wrong
So at night when I'm home and I start to feel alone
I don't call a close friend
I just reach out for my phone
And before the day ends
I will be inside a zone.

Shaken By Society

I saw a fight the other day
Got me thinking should I take a flight or should I stay
Should I step in between and make these problems go away
But the gangsters with the guns saying that they going to spray
So I take a step back, fix my hat and take a breath
America's the cause of every human beings death
The sights that I see makes the thoughts turn to me
And now I'm looking up at God like what am I going to be?
Will I be a rap star or a drug trap star?
Walking down the street left a permanent scar
Save me from this nightmare
And if not I understand
My reality's dream
God wake me if you can

Hidden Thoughts

Life never fails to amaze

My friends breaking down weed trying to get blazed

I refuse to get high because I'm already dazed

And there's nothing but poetry helping me out of this phase

I want to do right but my thoughts seem to drift

Feel the darkness of the night

And my mind takes a shift

Trying to stay high but can't seem to find a lift

I'm just hoping that I make it

And do something with this gift

That I acquire

Writing poetry is a passion

A burning desire

The words cut through your soul like cuts from a wire

Get a deal, make a sell, I'm in need of a buyer

Seal the deal

Live life well and then I'll retire.

More Thoughts

Everything in life is so wrong
A thousand kids a day blowing drugs out of a bong
I can't help but notice that the youth has gone astray
I turn my thoughts into a song
And a song into a home where everybody can stay
And all the children can play
I think that we all could use more love and less violence
A boy getting beat and his presence strikes a silence
I begin to hate the world every day I get defiant
Because this life is so crazy I don't want to wake up
My food for thought is getting old
I need new stuff to bake up
I need to free my thoughts that I think about the youth
So I turn to the poetry
The spitting image of the truth

What Happens?

What happens when you grow without a father?
What happens when your son don't care so he don't even bother?
What happens when he starts to feel as if he is about to go insane?
What happens when he takes that gun and puts it to his brain?
What happens when his mom is left to mourn and cry?
What happens when you leave this earth in search to find the sky?
What happens when you start to hate everything you love?
What happens when you swore that they would always be above?
What happens when you start to feel you're going to lose your mind?
What happens when you start to wish it was all just left behind?
What happens when you want a job but it's you they won't employ?
There are only three words
You eventually destroy.

Wishful Thinking

I wish that I could have her here
I wish that I could have her near
I wish that I could hold her close and softly whisper in her ear
I wish that I could tell her that I love her to death
But I played too many games and stole her heart
Call it theft
Right from the start
I wish that I could love
I wish that I could feel for you
I wish I was above
I'm wishing for a meal
I wish to fly just like a dove
I'm wishing for a lot
And I know you're wishing too
But the only difference is
My biggest wish is to have you.

Deep Inner Thoughts

I see a blind man with a cane
And a walking dog
I'm thinking he can't see so will he ever go insane?
His dog jerks away and starts to take a jog
And almost hits a speedy train
The blind man reaches out and grabs it and blows a breath of fog
That was close.
I see a blind man
Trapped in rain
Begging for a room
He wants to be inside before the thunder gives a boom
No one gives him money so you guess what he will do
He pulls a switch blade and it's you that he pursues
And as I sit up in this car
And wish upon a shooting star
I slowly take a break from life
Trying to stop from feeling blue

Tragic to Magic

The pain that was running through my brain
Had me feeling so insane
Looking out my window pane
Thinking will things be the same
Or will they forever remain
I'm staring out at the rain
Thinking should I just hop aboard the next train
Or pack my bag and go and take a plane
Or should I stay in my lane
Because when you run away
There's nothing that you can gain
Everything isn't tragic
And if you have a tragedy, then turn it into magic
Have them calling you "your majesty"
And you won't have to explain what's going on in your brain
Not saying you will have fame
Or money you can attain
I'm just saying that you'll have some peace inside your mind
Yeah, sit down and rewind
To recent memories and good times
And how you made it through when life was throwing lemons and limes
And life wasn't finer than wine
But you made it
You are divine
So shine
And realize that no matter what you are fine

My Story

I AM HERE!

The first day I grabbed those pills I felt like I had power. Something magical was brewing inside of me. Did I think that I was powerful for making the brutal decision to be a coward and take the easy way out of life? Did I think that by ending my life and causing pain upon many of people would make society a better place? As silly as it may seem, that's exactly what I thought. I thought that it was perfectly fine to let the world label me as another black man dying by his own hand. But it wasn't. You see what I learned is that life has it's moments, and sometimes things get so low you want to give up, but that's when you have to let go and let God take control of things.

There is no such thing as an easy way out. People kill themselves thinking that it ends everything and that the pain goes away, but it doesn't. What you run away from in your current life, you will most definitely deal with in the afterlife. Often people get so stuck inside of the moment that they forget to take a step back and just realize the blessings that God has given them.

Well I took that step back to just realize, and I will keep doing it. But I wasn't always living with this mindset. There was a time when my spirit was so broken, and I just hated everyone and everything around me. Everything was lies, and everyone was out to get me. My mindset was so depressing that I didn't want to live with it anymore. I wanted to be dead. That's right. If someone would have given me a gun, I probably would have pulled the trigger. It's amazing because I was only 15 years old at the time. What could be so bad that I would want to kill myself? I could have spent hours reasoning why I could have killed myself, but now, two years later, I can honestly say that their is nothing that could be bad enough to make me want to die. At the end of the day I have my loving family, and the bible. Nothing can defeat me. Forever here is where I will be. I am Justin Young, not your average 17 year old kid. But I am here. *I AM HERE and not going anywhere.*

Justin's I AM Story was featured on http://aliveonpurpose.tumblr.com by Alive on Purpose, an organization dedicated to bringing awareness to suicide prevention and purpose discovery! Please show your support by visiting them at http://www.imaliveonpurpose.com.

About the Author

Justin is a 17 year old senior at Lyons Township High School in LaGrange, Illinois. In 2010, he went through a bout of depression that would send him on a downward spiral for two years with an attempt at taking his own life. Through strained relationships, increased academic struggles, and many other negative experiences, this poet's journey was born.

This booklet "A Poet's Journey" was written out of those dark times and published by the grace and restoration of God's and a family's love. Justin would like teens everywhere to know, you are not alone, but there is HOPE!

For speaking engagements, please contact Justin at:

theyoungcorp@att.net

www.ingramcontent.com/pod-product-compliance
Lightning Source LLC
Chambersburg PA
CBHW071458070426
42452CB00040B/1884